WHAT *IS* FAITH?

The Crucial Questions Series
By R. C. Sproul

WHO *Is* JESUS?

CAN I TRUST *the* BIBLE?

DOES *Prayer* CHANGE THINGS?

CAN I *Know* GOD'S WILL?

HOW SHOULD I *Live* IN THIS WORLD?

WHAT DOES IT MEAN *to Be* BORN AGAIN?

CAN I BE SURE *I'm* SAVED?

WHAT *Is* FAITH?

WHAT CAN I *Do with* MY GUILT?

WHAT *Is the* TRINITY?

WHAT *Is* BAPTISM?

CAN I HAVE *Joy in* MY LIFE?

WHO IS *the* HOLY SPIRIT?

DOES GOD *Control* EVERYTHING?

Crucial
Questions
No. 8

WHAT *IS* FAITH?

R.C. SPROUL

Ɽ *Reformation Trust*   A DIVISION OF LIGONIER MINISTRIES, ORLANDO, FL

What Is Faith?

© 2010 by R. C. Sproul

Published by Reformation Trust Publishing
a division of Ligonier Ministries
421 Ligonier Court, Sanford, FL 32771
Ligonier.org   ReformationTrust.com

Printed in North Mankato, MN
Corporate Graphics
June 2016
First edition, eighth printing

Cover design: Gearbox Studios

Interior design and typeset: Katherine Lloyd, The DESK

Unless otherwise noted, Scripture quotations are from *The Holy Bible, English
Standard Version*®, copyright © 2001 by Crossway Bibles, a publishing ministry of
Good News Publishers. Used by permission. All rights reserved.

Scripture quotations marked NKJV are from the *New King James Version*®.
Copyright © 1982 by Thomas Nelson. Used by permission. All rights reserved.

Library of Congress Cataloging-in-Publication Data

Sproul, R. C. (Robert Charles), 1939-
  What is faith? / R. C. Sproul.
    p. cm. -- (The crucial questions series)
  Includes bibliographical references.
  ISBN 978-1-56769-207-5
1. Faith. 2. Reformed Church--Doctrines. I. Title.
BT771.3.S68 2010
231'.042--dc22

                        2010011554

Contents

One—A Hopeful Vision 1

Two—Examples of Faith 19

Three—A Gift from God 45

Four—Strengthened by the Word 55

Chapter One

A Hopeful
Vision

When we talk about Christianity, we are more likely to call it the "Christian faith" than the "Christian religion." This is appropriate in that the concept of faith is fundamental to Christianity because faith is central to the biblical view of redemption. Yet faith is a many-faceted concept, so even many professing Christians struggle to understand exactly what it is.

In this booklet, I want to explore the nature of faith as it is defined in the Bible. We will focus on how faith relates to our salvation and will discuss the necessary ingredients of what we call "saving faith." We'll also look at how faith relates to reason and at other issues that we encounter in the Bible with respect to this concept.

Faith Is the Substance of Hope

The most foundational definition for faith in the Bible is found in Hebrews: "Now faith is the substance of things hoped for, the evidence of things not seen. For by it the elders obtained a good testimony" (11:1–2, NKJV). Note the distinction the author of Hebrews makes between faith and hope. These ideas are intimately connected, but they are distinct nonetheless. In a similar way, Paul writes in 1 Corinthians 13 of the great triad of Christian virtues: faith, hope, and love. This passage also reveals that there is a distinction between faith and hope.

Before we explore the link between these concepts, let me address the biblical idea of hope, because the word *hope* functions somewhat differently in the New Testament than it does in Western countries today. When we use the word *hope*, we usually are referring to an emotional state of desire in our hearts regarding what we would like to happen in the future but are not sure will come to pass. We may hope that our favorite teams will win football or basketball games, but that hope may never materialize. For instance, I am a perennial fan of the Pittsburgh Steelers, and I regularly hope that the Steelers will win their football games. This may be a vain and futile hope because it's anything but a certainty. There is a kind of hope that does not make us ashamed (cf. Rom. 5:5), but I'm constantly afraid that my hopes for the Steelers may make me ashamed, for while they regularly win championships, they lose games, too.

However, when the Bible speaks of hope, it is not referring to a desire for a future outcome that is uncertain, but rather a desire for a future outcome that is absolutely sure. Based on our trust in the promises of God, we can be fully confident about the outcome. When God gives His people a promise for the future, and the church grasps it, this hope is said to be the "anchor of the soul" (Heb. 6:19). An anchor is that which gives a ship protection against aimless drifting in the sea. The promises of God for tomorrow are the anchor for believers today.

When the Bible says "faith is the *substance* of things hoped for" (Heb. 11:1, emphasis added), it is speaking of something that has weight or significance—something of extreme value. The implication is that faith communicates the essence of the hope.

In a real sense, hope is faith looking forward. The word *faith* carries a strong element of trust. If my hope is based on something God has said will happen in the future, the hope I have for that future promise finds its substance from my trust and confidence in the One making the promise. I can have hope because I have faith in God. Because I can trust the promise of God for tomorrow, there is substance to my hope; my hope is not just a chimera, a fantasy, or a wish projection based on idle dreams. Rather, it is based on something substantive.

Faith Is the Evidence of Things Not Seen

The definition of faith continues: "faith is . . . the evidence of things not seen." The author uses a reference to one of the senses of the human body through which we gain knowledge, the sense of sight. There is a popular expression today, "Seeing is believing." Similarly, people from Missouri like to say, "Show me." This attitude is not opposed to biblical faith, for the New Testament calls us to put our trust in the gospel not on the basis of some irrational leap into the darkness but on the basis of the testimony of eye-witnesses who report in Scripture about what they saw.

Think, for example, of the apostolic testimony of Peter: "For we did not follow cleverly devised myths when we made known to you the power and coming of our Lord Jesus Christ, but we were eyewitnesses of his majesty" (2 Peter 1:16). Likewise, when Luke begins his Gospel, he addresses it to Theophilus, saying, "it seemed good to me . . . , having followed all things closely for some time past, to write an orderly account for you" (v. 3). He is talking about things he has substantiated on the basis of eyewitness testimony. In the same way, when Paul defends his confidence in the resurrection in 1 Corinthians 15, he appeals to the eyewitnesses of the risen Christ: Cephas, the Twelve, the five hundred, James, and all the apostles (vv. 5–7). Then he writes, "Last of all, as to one untimely born, he appeared also to me" (v. 8). Paul is saying, "I believe in the resurrection because many eyewitnesses saw the resurrected Christ, and I saw Him myself."

So there is a link in the New Testament between faith and seeing, and yet the author of Hebrews describes faith as the conviction of things *not* seen. Maybe this is why some people argue that there is a biblical ground for regarding blind faith as virtuous. After all, if one cannot see, one is said to be blind, so if faith is evidence for that which cannot be seen, that must mean that the faith of which the author is speaking is blind faith.

I cannot think of anything that is farther from the meaning of Hebrews 11:1–2 than blind faith. Those promoting blind faith say: "We believe what we believe for no reason whatsoever. It's totally gratuitous." The idea is that there's some kind of virtue in closing our eyes, taking a deep breath, and wishing with all of our might that something is true—then saying, "It's true." That is credulity, not faith.

The Bible never claims that we should jump into the darkness. In fact, the biblical injunction is for people to come out of the darkness and into the light (cf. John 3:19). Faith is not blind in the sense of being arbitrary, whimsical, or a mere expression of human desire. If that were the case, why would the author of Hebrews say that faith is "the evidence of things not seen"?

When faith is linked to hope, it is put into the time frame of the future, and the one thing that I cannot see at all is tomorrow. None of us has yet experienced tomorrow. As I said earlier, I have hope that the Pittsburgh Steelers will win their football games. But I cannot know in advance whether that will happen or not.

However, Hebrews says that faith is the *evidence* of things not seen. Evidence is tangible. Evidence is something we can know through our five senses. Evidence is what police officers inspect and try to collect at a crime scene—fingerprints, traces of gunpowder residue, articles of clothing that are left behind, and so on. All these things are visible and point beyond themselves to some important truth. That's why people analyze evidence.

The idea is this: I don't know what tomorrow is going to bring, but I know that God knows what tomorrow is going to bring. So if God promises that tomorrow will bring something, and if I trust God for tomorrow, I have faith in something I have not yet seen. That faith serves as evidence because its object is God. I know Him; He has a track record—He is infallible and never lies. God knows everything and is perfect in whatever He communicates. So if God tells me that something is going to happen tomorrow, I believe it even though I haven't seen it yet.

That's not credulity or irrationality. On the contrary, it is irrational *not* to believe something that God says regarding some future event.

What does God say regarding the future? He not only reveals to us events of tomorrow that we haven't yet seen, He also reveals to us much about the supernatural realm that our eyes cannot penetrate. We cannot see angels at this time. We cannot see heaven. But God reveals to us the reality of these things, and by faith we see that they have substance because God is credible.

Faith Is Believing God

When God came to Abraham, who is known as "the father of the faithful" (see Rom. 4:16), He spoke to him about the future. He said: "Go from your country and your kindred and your father's house to the land that I will show you. And I will make of you a great nation, and I will bless you and make your name great, so that you will be a blessing. I will bless those who bless you, and him who dishonors you I will curse, and in you all the families of the earth shall be blessed" (Gen. 12:1–3).

Abraham believed God. He set out, not knowing where he was going, journeying to a country and a future he had never seen. The New Testament tells us that "he was looking forward to the city that has foundations, whose designer and builder was God" (Heb. 11:10).

Abraham was not a prospector looking for hidden treasure based on a legend about pirate plunder hidden in a cave somewhere. Abraham was looking for a place because God had told him that He was going to show him that place. He trusted God for what he had not yet seen, and by doing that became the father of the faithful.

Like Abraham, we are pilgrims and sojourners in this world, searching for that heavenly country, the city whose designer and builder is God. We have not seen this city, but we know it exists, and the evidence for it is the trust that we have in the One who promises to bring it to pass.

At its root, this is what faith is. It is not believing *in* God. It's believing *God*. The Christian life is about believing God. It is about living by every word that proceeds from His mouth (Deut. 8:3; Matt. 4:4). It is about following Him into places where we've never been, into situations that we've never experienced, into countries that we've never seen—because we know who He is.

This is the kind of faith that the Bible calls, in one sense, childlike faith; not *childish* but *childlike*. When we were infants, we had very little knowledge about what was safe and what was dangerous. We would put our hands up into the hands of our fathers or mothers, and they would take us down the street. When we came to a corner, we didn't know the difference between a red light and a green light. But they guided us. When they stopped, we stopped. When they stepped off the curb and crossed the street, so did we. We trusted our parents because we were under their care.

Sadly, there are parents who are so corrupt that they violate the trust that their small children give to them. These parents beat their children and sometimes even kill them. Nevertheless, a child's trust in his or her mother and father is not an irrational thing in most cases. By analogy, we are called to trust God, to know that He is looking out for us. He's not going to lead us into disaster. Childlike faith has confidence in the character of the God who regards us as His children.

The pilgrimage of the Christian life is a pilgrimage of faith. It begins when God creates faith in our hearts. In the first stage of our Christian experience, we embrace Christ and trust Him for our redemption, but the whole pilgrimage of the Christian is rooted and grounded in that confidence, that trust. The whole process is defined by living in faith (cf. Col. 2:6). That's why God told the prophet Habakkuk, "the righteous shall live by his faith."

Habakkuk was mystified that God would allow His chosen people to be defeated by a pagan nation and be put in a state of oppression. Habakkuk said that he would go up on his watchtower and wait for God to declare Himself. He writes:

> I will take my stand at my watchpost and station myself on the tower, and look out to see what he will say to me, and what I will answer concerning my complaint. And the Lord answered me: "Write the vision; make it plain on tablets, so he may run who reads it. For still the vision awaits its appointed time; it hastens to the end—it will not lie. If it seems slow, wait for it; it will surely come; it will not delay. Behold, his soul is puffed up; it is not upright within him, but the righteous shall live by his faith." (Hab. 2:1–4)

This seemingly innocuous statement, "the righteous shall live by his faith," is quoted three times in the New Testament

(Rom. 1:17; Gal. 3:11; Heb. 10:38); it is a central motif in the writings of Paul. It means that God is pleased when His people live by trusting Him.

God tells Habakkuk: "I will answer your question. But I will not answer it immediately. You must wait. But while you wait, remember that the answer will surely come." Then He makes the contrast to the proud person, who is not upright, who lives according to his sight, by what's immediately in front of him. He has no time for trusting the invisible promises of God. In stark contrast is the man of faith. Even though God's promises tarry, they are sure to come to pass, and the righteous person in God's sight is the person who lives by faith.

This expression, "the righteous shall live by his faith," is translated by Jesus in His conflict with Satan in the wilderness when Jesus reminds the Devil that man does not live by bread alone but by every word that proceeds from the mouth of God (Matt. 4:4). To say that we live by all the words that God speaks is the same thing as saying that we live by faith. We take God at His word. We trust our lives, body and soul, to Him, to His value system, to His structure, and to His Word.

Faith and Evidence

As he continues to unfold the meaning of faith, the author of Hebrews turns our attention to one of the most astounding sights that our eyes can behold: the universe we live in. We read: "By faith we understand that the universe was created by the word of God, so that what is seen was not made out of things that are visible" (Heb. 11:3). That's a somewhat complicated sentence, but note that the divine origin of creation is embraced by an act of faith, not by an act of credulity.

Many people think that the conflict today between science and religion is a conflict between reason and irrationality. But the Bible does not call us to believe in the divine act of creation simply through a leap of faith or by a crucifixion of the intellect by which we ignore what reason can teach us. The great theologians of church history—people like Augustine and Thomas Aquinas, for example—distinguished between faith and reason but insisted that what is embraced by faith is never irrational.

Neither are faith and reason antithetical. Both Augustine and Aquinas believed that all truth is God's truth, and that all truth meets at the top. God reveals His truth not only through the Bible, but also through what we call "natural revelation." Genesis 1–2 shows us that God is the Creator of all things, but also, "The heavens declare the glory of God, and the sky above proclaims his handiwork" (Ps. 19:1).

In his epistle to the Romans, Paul tells us that God's invisible attributes—they're invisible in the sense we cannot see them—can be perceived through the things that have been made (Rom. 1:20). In other words, a knowledge of the invisible God is revealed to us through that which is visible. The creation itself screams out the reality of the Creator. Therefore, there should be no conflict in our understanding of the nature of the universe and our understanding of the origin of the universe, which no one has seen.

Many years ago, I engaged in correspondence with Dr. Carl Sagan, the late astronomer and astrophysicist, when we both responded to a publication on questions of theology and philosophical cosmogony. We talked about the "Big Bang" theory that he was espousing. Sagan said that through the scientific apparatus, we can now go back to within a nanosecond of the moment of the Big Bang. I replied: "Well, let's go back before that. What was there, in your judgment, before this explosion? You have said there was a complete concentration of all matter and energy into an infinitesimal point of singularity, a point that had been in a state of organization and inertia for eternity, but which suddenly decided to blow up. I want to know who moved it. I want to know what outside force perturbed its inertia." He said: "Well, we can't go there. We don't need to go there." I said, "Yes, you *do* need to go there, because if you assume that the Big Bang happened gratuitously, you're talking about magic, not science."

The point is that no scientist was present as an observer for that event. There were no eyewitnesses of the creation. So we come to the origin of the universe through some kind of deduction from the things that we see, or we look to the supernatural revelation that God gives us, which antedates the material universe as we know it. I believe that we come to the same conclusion either way.

Hebrews tells us, "By faith we understand that the universe was created by the word of God, so that what is seen was not made out of things that are visible" (11:3). That's like saying, "The things that are seen did not come from things that are seen." At some point in your scientific analysis, as you reason backward from what you can see, you run up against the causal necessity of an unseen, invisible, nonphysical cause for all that you see. That's why historically Christian theologians have spoken of "creation *ex nihilo*"—creation *out of nothing*.

Of course, that does not mean that nothing was involved, because God is a something and not a nothing. An eternal, self-existent being was the efficient cause of the universe. He brought it into being. The idea behind *ex nihilo* is simply that God did not merely rearrange or reshape preexisting matter as a potter forms clay into an attractive vessel. Instead, God brought the physical world into being from nothing. Had God brought the world into existence out of preexisting matter, that matter would have required a *material* cause, and that material itself would have required a material cause, and so on, all the way back into eternity, which is absurd. No, "what is seen was not made out of things that are visible."

So when Hebrews 11:3 says that we understand creation by faith, it means that we are to trust the Word of God at this point. We were not there at the creation, but God was, and He has given us an account of it. He says: "Here's how it happened. I commanded the universe into being. I am who I am. I have the power of being in and of Myself. I am eternal. I am the Author of the non-eternal existence of a finite universe. It came into being through My creative power. I said, 'Let there be light,' and there was light."

We trust God's Word to understand that the world in which we live was designed, framed, and created by the Word of God, so that the things that are seen were not made of things that were (or are) visible. We cannot find anything in the universe today that has, in itself, sufficient power to account for its existence. In fact, the more we analyze it, the more finite and contingent it manifests itself to be.

Chapter Two

EXAMPLES
OF FAITH

As an existential philosopher and a Christian, Søren Kierkegaard was somewhat negative toward nineteenth-century European culture. He once said, "Let others complain that our age is evil; my complaint is that it is paltry."[1] He meant that his era was a time when people lacked passionate faith. To relieve his discouragement, he

---

1 Søren Kierkegaard, *Either/Or: A Fragment of Life* (London: Penguin Books, 1992), 48.

went back to the pages of the Old Testament: "There at least one feels that it's human beings talking. There people hate, people love, people murder their enemy and curse his descendants through all generations, there people sin."[2] He was not rejoicing in these sinful behaviors. He merely was noting that the Old Testament saints exercised their faith amid real-life turmoil and struggle.

Like Kierkegaard, I turn to the stories in the pages of the Old Testament to see flesh-and-blood examples of what it means to live by faith. The author of the letter to the Hebrews did the same, collecting many of these examples in the so-called hall of fame of heroes and heroines of faith (Heb. 11:4–40). As we consider these examples, we learn much about the nature of faith.

Abel: Giving Honor to God

The hall of fame of faith begins with one of the earliest men of God: "By faith Abel offered to God a more acceptable sacrifice than Cain, through which he was commended as righteous, God commending him by accepting his gifts.

---

2 Ibid.

And through his faith, though he died, he still speaks" (Heb. 11:4).

Here we see that faith is not simply trusting God for the future or trusting the Word of God for the truth about things that are invisible to our eyes, even things that happened in the past, such as the creation. Faith is also the means by which we live in response to the commands of God.

We are told that Abel offered a more excellent sacrifice than Cain. We read in the book of Genesis how both Cain and Abel offered their sacrifices to God (4:3–7). God received the sacrifice of Abel but rejected the one from Cain. Some people argue that the reason for the difference in God's response was that Abel offered an animal sacrifice while Cain offered produce of the fields, but nothing in the Bible says that only an animal offering is acceptable to God. All kinds of occasions for grain offerings, cereal offerings, and others are set forth in the Old Testament, so it is not appropriate for us to conclude that God accepted Abel's sacrifice and rejected Cain's because of the nature of the sacrifices themselves. Instead, Abel is commended here in Hebrews 11 not because he gave an animal but because he offered his sacrifice by faith.

God was very concerned, as we see throughout the Old Testament, with the heart attitude of the person who brought a sacrifice to the altar. Very often in the Old Testament era, people simply went through the motions, offering their sacrifices in a perfunctory way, for which they were hypocrites. God said, "I hate, I despise your feasts, and I take no delight in your solemn assemblies" (Amos 5:21). God was displeased by the faithlessness of the people as they went through their religious practices. Yet that happens in every generation. People go to church every Sunday and go through the motions of religion while their hearts are far from God. They act out their religion, as actors in a play, but without faith, without any real personal commitment to God.

But when Abel brought his sacrifice, he brought it with the sacrifice of praise. He wanted to honor God. He was trying to be obedient and to manifest his love for God and trust in Him. It was a genuine act of worship. But Cain brought a sacrifice in a hypocritical fashion. In fact, we see the true character of Cain immediately thereafter. He became jealous because God received the sacrifice of his brother, so he rose up in a jealous rage and killed Abel.

Cain was a faithless man, as he demonstrated by his evil deed. But Abel's life was marked by faith.

Enoch: Pleasing God

In Hebrews 11:5 we read, "By faith Enoch was taken up so that he should not see death, and he was not found, because God had taken him. Now before he was taken he was commended as having pleased God." This vignette builds on that of Abel. Enoch was translated (bypassing physical death) because he pleased God. The author of Hebrews then explains the connection to faith: "And without faith it is impossible to please him, for whoever would draw near to God must believe that he exists and that he rewards those who seek him" (v. 6).

We cannot come to God if we don't believe there is a God. That's simple, isn't it? We cannot seek to please God if we don't believe that God exists and rewards those who seek after Him. Enoch demonstrated his faith by seeking to please God, just as all faithful people do. So faith is central to the motivation of the human heart to live in a way that honors God.

We see this in the Gospels as well. When Jesus met people who went out of their way to show honor to Him, He commended them for their faith. This was because no one bothers to honor a person he doesn't believe exists or is worthy of honor.

Opinion polls continue to indicate that a very high percentage of people in the United States believe in the existence of God, but the figure is essentially meaningless. Usually the question is stated something like this: "Do you believe in a supreme being, a higher power, or something greater than yourself?" Anybody can believe in a higher power. Cosmic dust is a higher power. But it's not God. When the pollsters probe further by asking, "Do you want to please God and live for Him?" the number of positive responses becomes much smaller.

So many of us are practical atheists. We may be theoretical theists, but our lives betray a practical kind of atheism in that we don't live in order to please God. If we don't live in order to please God, it can only be because we do not really believe He is worth our attention.

It has been said that if you want to find out what a person really believes, you should analyze his checkbook. As Jesus said, "Where your treasure is, there will your heart be also" (Luke 12:34). So if you want to know where your heart is, check out your treasure. Do we invest in the kingdom of God or our own kingdoms? The person who lives by faith lives to please God, not men. Enoch was singled out because he had a consuming passion in his life to please God. That's what a person of faith does.

Noah: A Fool for Christ

The next hero of faith cited in Hebrews 11 is Noah: "By faith Noah, being warned by God concerning events as yet unseen, in reverent fear constructed an ark for the saving of his household. By this he condemned the world and became an heir of the righteousness that comes by faith" (v. 7). God warned Noah that He was going to send a massive deluge on the earth to destroy the human race because of its sin, but He commanded Noah to make a large boat to save his family and animal species (Gen. 6). "In reverent fear," Noah set about to do exactly what God commanded.

We know that it took Noah many years to build the ark, and many Bible scholars have made the point that Noah must have been ridiculed by the people of his time. Many years ago, I heard a comedy routine in which Bill Cosby played the role of Noah. As he was building the ark in the middle of the desert, his friends would come by and ask, "Noah, what are you doing?" He would reply, "Building a boat." "Why?" "Well, because there's going to be a flood." Cosby captured the ridicule that Noah likely experienced when he gave the response of the people: "Yeah, sure."

Building an ark in a desert is certainly ludicrous in and of itself. But Noah believed God, and he was willing to be what the New Testament speaks of as a "fool for Christ" (1 Cor. 4:10). He put his confidence not in the judgments of this world but in the judgment of God. He built the ark, through which the human race survived, because he lived by faith.

The Scriptures say that Noah's activity in this regard "condemned the world" (Heb. 11:7a). His faithfulness "showed up" the faithlessness of the other people of his day. Through this faith, he "became an heir of the righteousness that comes by faith" (v. 7b).

Abraham: Faith and Obedience

After discussing the faith of Abel, Enoch, and Noah, the author of Hebrews comes to Abraham. As I mentioned in the previous chapter, this man has been called "the father of the faithful." We read: "By faith Abraham obeyed when he was called to go out to a place that he was to receive as an inheritance" (Heb. 11:8). Notice that the word *faith* is conjoined here with the word *obeyed*. Living in submission to what God commands is the essence of faith. That is what Abraham did to a large degree, which is why he is called the father of the faithful. While Abraham was still living in paganism, God appeared to him and promised that he would be the father of a great nation. We are told that "he [Abraham] believed the Lord, and he counted it to him as righteousness" (Gen. 15:6).

Paul labors the point that Abraham represents the great example of a person who is justified by faith and not by works (Rom. 4:17). When a person embraces the promises of God that are found in Christ, that person is instantly justified. Even so Abraham was counted (or reckoned) righteous by God because he trusted the promise of God. Abraham then demonstrated his faith through obedience over time. That's why James would point later to Genesis 22, where Abraham offered up Isaac on the altar, demonstrating the fruit of his faith in obedience (James 2:21).

So the author of Hebrews says it was by faith that

Abraham obeyed when God called him to go to a place he did not know. Let's think about that. We can sensational-ize it and make it more pious than real, but the reality was that Abraham was an old man. He had his roots firmly established in Mesopotamia. That's where his family was. That's where his possessions were. That's where his heritage was. But then, in his old age, God came to him and said: "I want you to get out of this land. Get out of your place where you're culturally comfortable. I am going to make you an alien in a strange and foreign land. I'll show you where it is."

So Abraham packed up and left. If ever a venture was undertaken by faith alone, it was this immigration of Abra-ham to a foreign land. That's why we are told: "By faith he went to live in the land of promise, as in a foreign land, living in tents with Isaac and Jacob, heirs with him of the same promise. For he was looking forward to the city that has foundations, whose designer and builder is God" (Heb. 11:9–10).

There's something significant about the lifestyle of Abraham as a man of faith, as well as that of his son and grandsons. Abraham lived the life of a pilgrim. He didn't have a permanent address. He lived in a tent, which was also the experience of the people of Israel. They were semi-nomads. They moved all over the landscape as the weather patterns changed in order to ensure sustenance for their flocks. They had to go where the grass was growing at a particular time, so there was no permanent place they could call home. Abraham waited and looked for a city that was not an earthly city, but one whose builder was God.

But Abraham was looking for more than a land. Remember Jesus' words: "If you abide in my word, you are truly my disciples, and you will know the truth, and the truth will set you free" (John 8:31–32). The Pharisees took umbrage at that, responding, "We are offspring of Abraham and have never been enslaved to anyone" (v. 33). Jesus said: "If you were Abraham's children, you would be doing the works Abraham did. . . . Your father Abraham rejoiced that he would see my day. He saw it and was glad" (vv. 39, 56). Jesus was saying the same thing as the author of Hebrews: Abraham not only looked forward to the promise of land, he looked forward to the promise of the Redeemer, which promise was fulfilled in the person of Christ.

When Paul teaches the doctrine of justification by faith alone in his epistle to the Romans, his "Exhibit A," the person he uses to illustrate how salvation works, is Abraham.

He makes the point that people in the Old Testament were redeemed in exactly the same way as people are redeemed today. There was not one way of salvation in Israel and another way in the new covenant (Christian) community. Justification is by faith now; justification was by faith back then. The meritorious ground of salvation in the Old Testament was the merit of Christ, not the merit of bulls and goats. As we are told elsewhere in Hebrews, the blood of bulls and goats could never take away sin (Heb. 10:4, 11), but those sacrifices pointed beyond themselves (Heb. 9:13–14). They prefigured or foreshadowed the coming Messiah, whose blood would take away sin.

The only difference between Abraham and us is the direction of time. Abraham looked forward to the cross; we look backward to the cross. His faith was in the promise; our faith is in the fulfillment of that promise. But the way of salvation was the same for Abraham as it is for us today.

Sarah: Judging God to Be Faithful

The author of Hebrews goes on to speak of Abraham's wife, Sarah: "By faith Sarah herself received power to conceive, even when she was past the age, since she considered him faithful who had promised. Therefore from one man, and him as good as dead, were born descendants as many as the stars of heaven and as many as the innumerable grains of sand by the seashore" (11:11–12).

Like her husband, Sarah judged God to be faithful. That's the dynamic of faith. As I said above, faith is not believing that there is a God. Faith is believing God. Faith is trusting the fidelity of God. When I am faithful, I am relying on One whom I deem to be perfectly faithful. That's what Sarah did, and that's what people do today when they put their trust in God because they see that He alone is ultimately worthy of absolute trust.

There is a kind of interlude in the roll call in Hebrews 11:13–16: "These all died in faith, not having received the things promised, but having seen them and greeted them from afar, and having acknowledged that they were strangers and exiles on the earth. For people who speak thus make it clear that they are seeking a homeland. If they had been thinking of that land from which they had gone out, they would have had opportunity to return. But as it is, they desire a better country, that is, a heavenly one. Therefore God is not ashamed to be called their God, for he has prepared for them a city."

This passage sums up the experiences of those who already have been enumerated. They had much in common, including this: they died in faith. They died without seeing or realizing the full measure of the promises that made them pilgrims in the first place. God promised Abraham that he would be the father of a great nation. We talk about Canaan as the "promised land," and it was promised first of all to Abraham and to his seed, yet the only parcel of real estate that Abraham ever owned after he made his journey from Mesopotamia was Machpelah, which was the site of his grave. That was the only piece of property that he actually inherited, but he could see the future fulfillment of the promise that God made him, and he trusted in that.

Abraham: Trusting Resurrection Power

The author of Hebrews finds yet another aspect of the faith of Abraham, causing him to revisit the great patriarch: "By faith Abraham, when he was tested, offered up Isaac, and he who had received the promises was in the act of offering up his only son, of whom it was said, 'Through Isaac shall your offspring be named.' He considered that God was able even to raise him from the dead, from which, figuratively speaking, he did receive him back" (Heb. 11:17–19).

Apart from Christ's obedient sacrifice, probably the greatest act of faith in fear and trembling recorded in all of Scripture is the obedient response of Abraham when God commanded him to sacrifice his son Isaac. This occurred after God had given Abraham a promise of future generations through Isaac and after God had made him wait many years for the birth of Isaac. In the interim, Abraham had taken steps to make sure that this promise was fulfilled with the aid of his wife Sarah, who, regarding herself as barren, offered her handmaid Hagar as a surrogate mother so that Abraham could have a son in order to fulfill the promise. Hagar had a son named Ishmael—but he was not the son of promise. Finally, after more years of waiting, God opened the womb of Sarah, and in her old age and in her barrenness, she brought forth a son who was given the name *Isaac* (when told she would have a son, Sarah had laughed, and the name *Isaac* means "laughter" in the Hebrew language). All of Abraham's hopes, his entire destiny, was wrapped up in this child.

Then God came to him and said, "Take your son, your only son Isaac, whom you love, and go to the land of Moriah, and offer him there as a burnt offering on one of the mountains of which I shall tell you" (Gen. 22:2). Abraham, in fear and trembling, set out on that three-day journey with Isaac. On the way, Isaac asked Abraham, "Behold, the fire and the wood, but where is the lamb for a burnt offering?" (v. 7). Abraham responded, "God will provide for himself the lamb" (v. 8).

I think we can read this story and make Abraham a paper saint with a glib kind of piety, as if he were saying to Isaac, "Hey, don't worry about it, son, God's going to provide us with a lamb when we get to the mountain." Not at all. Abraham was shaking in his boots. He was wondering: "How could God ask me to do this? How could God call me to such a place at such a time to do such a thing?" But he trusted God, clearly assuming that after he killed Isaac, God would raise him up from the dead (Heb. 11:19).

So Abraham went to the mountain designated by God, built the altar, spread the wood, and bound his son. But when he raised the knife, at the last possible second, God intervened and said, "Do not lay your hand on the boy or do anything to him, for now I know that you fear God" (Gen. 22:12). This is a story of faith to the absolute degree.

The only thing that ever exceeds it in Scripture is the faith of Christ Himself.

Abraham's Descendants: A Legacy of Faith

The author of Hebrews next turns to Abraham's descendants. He writes: "By faith Isaac invoked future blessings on Jacob and Esau" (Heb. 11:20). Though Esau was Isaac's firstborn son, he despised his birthright and sold it to Jacob (Gen. 25:34), and Jacob by trickery and deceit received the greater blessing (Gen. 27:27–29), all in accordance with God's sovereign plan (Gen. 25:23). Hebrews then notes, "By faith Jacob, when dying, blessed each of the sons of Joseph, bowing in worship over the head of his staff" (11:21).

Then we encounter Joseph. Just one sentence is devoted to him: "By faith Joseph, at the end of his life, made mention of the exodus of the Israelites and gave directions concerning his bones" (11:22). If any character in the Old Testament lived by faith, it was Joseph, because most of the time he lived by faith he was all alone. He had no compatriots from the Jewish faith with him. He was in prison in an alien country, falsely accused, unjustly sentenced, all alone. But he trusted God in that cell until God not only caused him to be released but elevated him to the prime ministership of Egypt, the strongest nation in the world at that time.

He later invited his extended family to dwell in Egypt, but when he was dying, he knew that at some future day his clan would leave Egypt for the Promised Land. Why? Because he knew the promise, and he knew that Egypt was not that land. Therefore, anticipating the Israelites' exodus from Egypt long before it happened, in his last will and testament Joseph left instructions to have his bones carried out of Egypt and back to the Promised Land. Now that's faith. Joseph was saying: "I may not get there while I'm alive in this life, but I want my bones to be disinterred and reburied in the Promised Land. I know my people will go there one day because God has promised it."

Moses' Parents: Faith in Providence

In verse 23, the roll call of faith begins to approach the events of the exodus: "By faith Moses, when he was born, was hidden for three months by his parents, because they saw that the child was beautiful, and they were not afraid of the king's edict." Moses' parents exercised faith in the dark days of their slavery in Egypt. They exhibited tremendous faith in trusting their most prized possession to the providence of God.

Think of it: When Pharaoh decreed that every male Hebrew child was to be slain, Moses' mother hid her infant until his lungs developed to the point where his cries could be heard. Then she made a basket out of reeds, carefully covered it with pitch, placed her baby in this basket, set it adrift in a tributary of the Nile, and let it go. She let it float away under the care of divine Providence, and God caused the very daughter of Pharaoh to find this baby, adopt it as her own, and raise him as a prince in Pharaoh's court. What an incredible outcome to a mother's faith.

Moses: Looking to the Reward

When the author of Hebrews focuses on Moses himself, he writes: "By faith Moses, when he was grown up, refused to be called the son of Pharaoh's daughter, choosing rather to be mistreated with the people of God than to enjoy the fleeting pleasures of sin. He considered the reproach of Christ greater wealth than the treasures of Egypt, for he was looking to the reward" (11:24–26).

In this brief description, the author of Hebrews recounts the radically life-changing decision that Moses made. On what do we base our decisions? What is the value system by which we determine to go one way or another? Moses clearly had a decision to make, a decision that involved an antithesis. In order to choose one thing, he had to reject something else. In order to go in one direction, he had to repudiate the other direction. In his upbringing, he had enjoyed the riches of the palace, educational benefits, status, and privilege. He had a life of ease and luxury laid out before him as a young man raised in Pharaoh's court. But he came to a crossroads in his life, and he chose not to bask in the treasures of the house of Pharaoh. Instead, "He chose to be mistreated with the people of God."

When did he make this choice? It was when he saw one of his own people being brutally beaten by a slave master and rose up to defend the man. He crossed the line and killed the Egyptian, and from that moment he could not go back. He chose exile, banishment to the Midianite wilderness and abject poverty, rather than continued enjoyment of "the fleeting pleasures of sin."

No sin has ever made any person happy. Sin simply cannot bring happiness, but it can deliver pleasure, and when we confuse pleasure with happiness, we are wide open to the seduction of the enemy. But the pleasures of sin are fleeting. They pass quickly, and Moses had to make a decision between the present and eternity, between the passing pleasures of sin and the afflictions of Christ, which have value for all time.

I can imagine people approaching Moses in the Midianite wilderness, where he was eking out a subsistence living, and asking him: "You once lived in Pharaoh's court, right? What are you doing here?" He would have answered that question by saying, "I'm living by faith." As Hebrews puts it, "He considered the reproach of Christ greater wealth than the treasures of Egypt, for he was looking to the reward."

When I was in seminary, I was selected to give a sermon in the seminary chapel. I gave a message on sin. At the end of the sermon, I was greeted by two groups. First, there were my fellow students, who were congratulatory. Second, there was a group of professors, who were absolutely incensed. In fact, one of them physically threw me up against a wall and accused me of distorting the Bible.

I certainly did not want to be guilty of distorting the Scriptures, so I went to one of my other professors, whose opinion I trusted, and I asked: "So-and-so just told me that I distorted the Scriptures. Did I?" I was so upset I was shaking. I was scared to death. But then this professor beamed from ear to ear. He said, "Oh, how blessed you are!" I didn't feel very blessed and I told him so. He said: "Don't you realize that what you just proclaimed was the unvarnished Word of God, and you just stirred up the hornet's nest. People hated you for Christ's sake. You just tasted the reproach of Christ! That is the greatest treasure you could ever have."

The difference between my professor and me was that he believed that. I didn't. I just wanted to run for my life. I was just a rookie, but he understood the things of God, just as Moses did.

Our Topsy-Turvy World

The author of Hebrews continues, citing one example of faith after another:

> By faith [Moses] left Egypt, not being afraid of the anger of the king, for he endured as seeing him who is invisible. By faith he kept the Passover and

sprinkled the blood, so that the Destroyer of the firstborn might not touch them. By faith the people crossed the Red Sea as on dry land, but the Egyptians, when they attempted to do the same, were drowned. By faith the walls of Jericho fell down after they had been encircled for seven days. By faith Rahab the prostitute did not perish with those who were disobedient, because she had given a friendly welcome to the spies. And what more shall I say? For time would fail me to tell of Gideon, Barak, Samson, Jephthah, of David and Samuel and the prophets— who through faith conquered kingdoms, enforced justice, obtained promises, stopped the mouths of lions, quenched the power of fire, escaped the edge of the sword, were made strong out of weakness, became mighty in war, put foreign armies to flight. Women received back their dead by resurrection. Some were tortured, refusing to accept release, so that they might rise again to a better life. Others suffered mocking and flogging, and even chains and imprisonment. They were stoned, they were sawn in two, they were killed with the sword. They went about in skins of sheep and goats, destitute, afflicted, mistreated—of

whom the world was not worthy—wandering about
in deserts and mountains, and in dens and caves of
the earth. (Heb. 11:27–38)

We live in a topsy-turvy world where beggars ride on
horses and princes walk in rags. The people named in Hebrews
11 were those of whom the world was not worthy—the ones
who were sawn in two, stoned, afflicted, and tormented, and
lived in deserts, mountains, and caves. On top of all that,
they did not experience the fulfillment of God's promise
in their lives: "And all these, though commended through
their faith, did not receive what was promised, since God
had provided something better for us, that apart from us
they should not be made perfect" (vv. 39–40).

The author is saying that these saints had to wait for
us. Just imagine if God had finished the consummation of
His work of redemption fifty years ago, thirty years ago,
or ten years ago. How many of us would have missed the
kingdom? But for our sake our fathers endured these inde-
scribable horrors—and that's something that we need to
revisit regularly. We have cut ourselves off from the history of the church, from biblical history, and we take very

lightly the things that the fathers of our faith paid for with their lives, property, and health.

When I think of the price that was paid for the recovery of the gospel from darkness in the sixteenth century, and then think of the cavalier way with which these same issues are regarded at the beginning of the twenty-first century, I simply do not understand it. Either we do not grasp the sweetness of the gospel or we know nothing about the history of God's people. There's a real sense in which the blood of our fathers screams at us from the ground today because we are not willing to make the same sacrifices that they made for us, and God will not honor a church composed of cowards.

If the church is ever to be the church triumphant, she must first be the church militant. She must be willing to enter into a spiritual war, one that could cost us our very lives. However, if we look at church history, we can see that the gospel radiated with its greatest clarity and brightness in those eras when the proponents of the faith spent most of their time in prison. But we enjoy the comforts of this world so much that we would rather have them than to live like those who were pilgrims and sojourners on the earth.

There's a conclusion to this roll call of faith in Hebrews 11, but it comes at the beginning of chapter 12. I always wonder how a chapter can start with the word *therefore,* because this word indicates the conclusion of what has come before it, but that is what happens in Hebrews 12. Here is the conclusion for our benefit: "Therefore, since we are surrounded by so great a cloud of witnesses, let us also lay aside every weight, and sin which clings so closely, and let us run with endurance the race that is set before us, looking to Jesus, the founder and perfecter of our faith" (Heb. 12:1–2a).

Isn't it interesting that after looking at all of these earthly heroes and heroines, the author of Hebrews says at the end, "Let's really look to the one who is the founder and perfecter of our faith, 'who for the joy that was set before him endured the cross, despising the shame, and is seated at the right hand of the throne of God' (Heb. 12:2b)"? In the next chapter, we'll consider what it means for Jesus to be the founder and perfecter of our faith.

Chapter Three

A GIFT
FROM GOD

I once had a conversation with a waitress about how wonderful it is to live in Florida, particularly during the cold months of the year. This young lady indicated she was from the north, but, she said, "I wouldn't go back up north to save my soul." I said: "Well, you and I differ at this point. I have no desire to go back north either, but if it meant the saving of my soul, I wouldn't hesitate to go."

When we say, "I wouldn't do this or that to save my soul," we're speaking in a jocular fashion. I dare say those who use that phrase have not given any real thought to the literal meaning of their words. They are not making any kind of statement about their souls. They are simply using a popular expression.

But in the seventeenth century, the church and people in the wider culture were very much concerned with the salvation of the human soul. The Westminster Confession of Faith manifests this concern, setting forth the biblical requirements for salvation in some detail. In chapter 14, the confession lays out the key prerequisite for salvation. The title of the chapter is "Of Saving Faith," and it begins with these words: "The grace of faith, whereby the elect are enabled to believe to the saving of their souls, is the work of the Spirit of Christ in their hearts. . . ."

Take careful note of those first four words. The confession does not simply speak of faith. Rather, it calls our attention to "the grace of faith." It calls faith a grace because it comes to us as a gift from God—something that we cannot buy, earn, or merit in any way. The usual definition for grace that we have in theology is "God's unmerited or undeserved favor." So faith is a manifestation of the grace of God. Simply put, those who are saved are enabled or empowered to believe to the end of the salvation of their souls. Faith is not seen as an accomplishment of the human spirit. In fact, faith is not something that is naturally exercised by a fallen human being.

Herein lies the crux of the matter that provokes so much controversy in theology. On the one hand, God requires faith, and yet on the other hand, Scripture says that no one can exercise saving faith unless God does something supernaturally to empower or enable him to do so.

Grant What Thou Dost Command

This harkens back to the ancient controversy between the heretic Pelagius and Augustine of Hippo. Augustine wrote a prayer in which he said, "O Lord, grant what Thou dost command and command what Thou dost desire." Pelagius objected to the first part of the prayer. He asked, "Why would you ask God to grant or give you a gift of something that He requires?" Pelagius was essentially saying: "If God requires something from a person, that person must—if God is just—have the ability within himself to meet the requirements. Otherwise, God would be unrighteous." Pelagius' ultimate conclusion was that since God demands perfection from people, people must have the ability to be perfect without any assistance from divine grace. But Augustine was saying, "We cannot please God unless God helps us in some manner to meet His requirements."

The dispute was over the doctrine of original sin. Augustine was saying that God makes His requirements of people who are fallen, who have a corrupt nature, who lack the ability to create faith in their own hearts. Before Adam fell, he had the ability to respond in faith to God without the supernatural assistance of grace. But after the fall, according to Augustine, man lacks that ability, so grace is an absolute prerequisite for us to meet the requirements.

The theology of the Westminster Confession is Augustinian throughout. When it addresses saving faith, it is echoing the teaching of Augustine and the church throughout the ages, saying that the faith that is required to please God is not something that we can conjure up out of our own strength. If we are to have saving faith, God the Holy Spirit must change the disposition of our hearts.

Reformed theology speaks of the *ordo salutis*, or the "order of salvation," which is an analysis of the logical order of events that must happen in order for a person to be redeemed. For example, we say that we're justified by faith. That means that a logical prerequisite for justification is faith. So in the order of salvation, faith comes before justification. Faith is not the fruit of justification; justification is the fruit of faith. But what comes before faith? In the *ordo salutis*, the event that precedes faith is regeneration.

Regeneration is popularly known as "rebirth," "the new birth," or "being born again." It is the operation by which God the Holy Spirit supernaturally and divinely changes the disposition of our hearts. While we are in our fallen condition, the Old Testament says, we have hearts of stone and desire only evil continuously (cf. Ezek. 11:19–20; Gen. 6:5). In a similar way, the New Testament declares that we are spiritually dead (Eph. 2:1). Regeneration occurs when the Holy Spirit comes to a person who is spiritually dead and makes him spiritually alive. The result is that whereas his heart was like a stone (unfeeling and unresponsive to the things of God), it now pulses in response to the things of God due to the operation of the Spirit.

This is what Jesus was speaking of when he said to Nicodemus, "Unless one is born again he cannot see the kingdom of God" and "Unless one is born of water and the Spirit, he cannot enter the kingdom of God" (John 3:3, 5). The word *unless* indicates what we call a "necessary condition." Jesus was saying to Nicodemus, "Something has to happen to a human being in order for him to see the king-dom of God or enter the kingdom of God." This necessity that Jesus discussed with Nicodemus was the experience of being reborn of the Spirit.

Regeneration means "generated again." It's a new begin-ning, a new genesis. We are born into this world biologically alive but spiritually dead. In order to become spiritually alive, we need the supernatural work of God the Holy Spirit in our hearts.

The popular evangelical view of the matter is that if you want to be born again, you need to have faith. Therefore, the popular view is that faith comes before regeneration. This idea implies that, in our fallen condition, while we're still in the flesh, while we're still dead in sins and trespasses, we can believe in order to be made anew. But that idea seems to be on a collision course with everything the New Testament teaches about regeneration. If left to ourselves, in our spiritual deadness, we would never incline ourselves to the things of God. Just as Jesus said, "No one can come to me unless it is granted him by the Father" (John 6:65). The ultimate reason why some people respond in faith to the gospel and others do not is that some (and not others) are regenerated by the Holy Spirit.

The difficult aspect of this doctrine is that God the Holy Spirit does not quicken everybody. That's what causes so many to stumble over this idea. If saving faith is the gift of God the Holy Spirit, and if God requires that gift for salvation, why doesn't He give it to everyone?

Faith Requires Election

That brings us to the doctrine of election. Saving faith is linked to election in the first sentence of the Westminster Confession chapter "Of Saving Faith": "The grace of faith, whereby the elect are enabled to believe to the saving of their souls, is the work of the Spirit of Christ in their hearts. . . ." The statement indicates that not everyone is enabled to be a believer, but only those to whom God determines to give the gift of enablement. This is the essence of the doctrine of election.

When Paul explained this doctrine to the Romans, he anticipated a frustrated response. He wrote: "What shall we say then? Is there injustice on God's part? By no means!" (Rom. 9:14). We must remember that God has decreed that He will have mercy to whom He will have mercy, and that He is never required to give His gifts of grace equally to all people (cf. Ex. 33:19; Rom. 9:15). The greatest act of mercy that God performs is giving the gift of faith.

Ephesians 2 is one of the most important texts on this topic. Paul begins this chapter by writing, "And you were dead in the trespasses and sins in which you once walked, following the course of this world, following the prince of the power of the air, the spirit that is now at work in the sons of disobedience, among whom we all once lived in the passions of our flesh, carrying out the desires of the body and the mind, and were by nature children of wrath, like the rest of mankind" (Eph. 2:1–3). The apostle is saying that while Christians share a common, fallen, corrupted humanity with the whole human race, they have received this unspeakable benefit of being quickened, or made alive, by the grace of God, whereby they were redirected from walking according to the lusts of the flesh and the desires of the mind. In other words, believers were redeemed while they were still dead and while they were by nature children of wrath, just like everybody else.

But then Paul goes on to say: "But God, being rich in mercy, because of the great love with which he loved us, even when we were dead in our trespasses, made us alive together with Christ—by grace you have been saved—and raised us up with him and seated us with him in the heavenly places in Christ Jesus, so that in the coming ages he might show the immeasurable riches of his grace in kindness toward us in Christ Jesus" (vv. 4–7). Then comes this: "For by grace you have been saved through faith. And this is not your own doing; it is the gift of God" (v. 8).

A whole realm of theological controversy focuses on what Paul means when he says, "*This* is not your own doing." What is it that is not our own doing? Is it the grace that is not our own doing? Or is it the faith?

Many believers say: "I acknowledge that I cannot have faith without grace, and obviously grace is not something that comes from me; it comes from God. So I need to have the assistance of grace, but the reason why some people are saved and others are not is that some people say 'Yes' to the offer of grace and other people say 'No' to it." So a person can interpret this passage to mean that we are saved because we trust the offer of grace, which offer did not come from ourselves, but from God.

However, what is meant by "not your own doing"? Is it grace or is it faith?

According to all the rules of Greek grammar, there is only one possible answer to that question. In the grammatical structure of this text, the antecedent of the word *this* is the word *faith*. The apostle is saying that we are saved by grace through faith, and that this faith through which we are saved is not of ourselves but is the gift of God.

When we think about the riches of divine mercy by which we were redeemed and contemplate that even the faith by which we are saved came not from our own flesh and will, but as a direct result of supernatural intervention in our lives, we ought to be driven to our knees in gratitude and thanksgiving.

We all have the same story when it comes down to it experientially. We know that we did not embrace Christ out of our flesh. We know that it took the inner work of God the Holy Spirit to change us from those who were opposed to the things of God to those who embrace the things of God. He made us alive and gave us the gift of faith by which we trust Christ.

Chapter Four

STRENGTHENED
BY THE WORD

John Wesley, the founder of Methodism, testified that his conversion experience occurred after he was already an ordained clergyman. He was at a meeting in Aldersgate Street in London, listening to a sermon from the book of Romans, and as he heard the words of Scripture—words he had heard many times before—he suddenly felt his heart "strangely warmed." He credited that event as his conversion to Christ.

Similarly, Augustine, while living a life of unbridled licentiousness, heard children playing a game in the garden with the refrain, "*Tolle lege, tolle lege*," or "Pick up and read." He looked up and saw a manuscript of the text of Romans. When he opened it, his eyes fell on the text of Romans 13:13–14: "Let us walk properly as in the daytime, not in orgies and drunkenness, not in sexual immorality and sensuality, not in quarreling and jealousy. But put on the Lord Jesus Christ, and make no provision for the flesh, to gratify its desires." The Word of God suddenly penetrated his heart, and he responded to the gospel.

In my own conversion experience, a young man quoted to me a verse from the book of Ecclesiastes: "If the clouds are full of rain, they empty themselves on the earth, and if a tree falls to the south or to the north, in the place where the tree falls, there it will lie" (11:3). I'm probably the only person in history who has been converted through that particular verse, but that image of a tree lying dead on the floor of the forest—inert, rotting, no longer producing fruit, worthless—gave me a picture of my life. I saw myself as a rotten tree, and God used that verse to quicken me to saving faith.

All of these conversion experiences, as different as they are, have one thing in common—the role of the Word of God. Many thousands, if not millions, of believers can also testify how the Holy Spirit worked in their lives through the sharp, penetrating power of the Word. The Scriptures are absolutely key in the process by which the Spirit gives—and strengthens—the faith of Christians.

Election and Adoption

In the previous chapter, we looked at Ephesians 2, where Paul shows that faith is a gift of God. In the first chapter of the epistle, Paul unmistakably links divine election and our adoption by God. The opening verses of Ephesians read: "Blessed be the God and Father of our Lord Jesus Christ, who has blessed us in Christ with every spiritual blessing in the heavenly places, even as he chose us in him before the foundation of the world, that we should be holy and blameless before him. In love he predestined us for adoption as sons through Jesus Christ, according to the purpose of his will, to the praise of his glorious grace, with which he has blessed us in the Beloved" (Eph. 1:3–6).

Election is the sovereign predestinating work of God,

the supreme expression of His mercy and grace. It is the act whereby, from all eternity, God determined to make some people, in Christ, to be His workmanship, crafted to be conformed to the image of Christ, to His glory, according to His sovereign will, and according to His plan to make us accepted before Him. After all, without faith we are not acceptable to God, but God makes us acceptable to Him through the gift of faith, leading to our justification. So in this section, Paul is talking about the glory of God's grace and mercy in that He meets these requirements.

In verse 13 of chapter 1, Paul makes this comment: "In him you also, when you heard the word of truth, the gospel of your salvation, and believed in him, were sealed with the promised Holy Spirit." So we are reborn, we hear the Word of God, we believe, we are justified, we are adopted, and we are sealed by the Holy Spirit. All of these things are part of the order of God's work of redemption in us.

What I especially want to point out in Ephesians 1:13 is the link between trusting Christ and hearing the Word of God. In the previous chapter, we looked at part of the Westminster Confession chapter "Of Saving Faith." That statement read: "The grace of faith, whereby the elect are enabled to believe to the saving of their souls, is the work of the Spirit of Christ in their hearts. . . ." But the statement doesn't end there; it continues by saying, ". . . and is ordinarily wrought by the ministry of the Word." This echoes the biblical statement that "faith comes from hearing, and hearing through the word of Christ" (Rom. 10:17).

We already have seen that faith comes by regeneration, the work of the Holy Spirit in the soul. But the ordinary way in which God the Holy Spirit operates on spiritually dead people and gives them the gift of faith is through the preaching of the Word. There is a distinction in the New Testament between the Word and the Spirit, but never a separation—the Spirit works with the Word and through the Word, never against the Word. God powerfully attends the proclamation of His Word with the work of the Holy Spirit. The Spirit inspired the Word when it originally was written. Today, He uses it to illumine us, and He applies it to our souls and hearts.

So faith is a gift from God, engendered by the Holy Spirit, and the ordinary way in which it is given is through the Word. Jesus said He would send the Holy Spirit to convict us of truth, of righteousness, and of sin (John 16:7–11), and He does that through His Word.

Seeking through Listening

Paul's connection of saving faith and God's eternal plan of election causes great confusion for many people. Someone once asked me: "Why should I listen to preachers or go to church? If I'm elect, I'm saved; if I'm not, I'm not, so there's nothing I can do." I replied: "You can know in this life that you are elect. You can make your calling and election sure, as the apostle Peter tells us, but you *cannot* know for sure in this world that you're *not* elect, because every person who is elect and has come to saving faith had a period in his life when he was not in faith." I gave him the example of Wesley, who, before his heart was "strangely warmed," may have thought that he wasn't elect since he wasn't a believer and his election had not yet been realized. Likewise, Augustine's election was not realized until he picked up a Bible and read that passage from Romans in the garden. A person may not come to saving faith until he is on his deathbed, and there really are such things as deathbed conversions. So even if a person is out of faith for his whole lifetime, that is not proof positive that he is not numbered among the elect.

This person continued: "Since I can't generate the faith

on my own, why should I bother? Why should I go to church?" I said, "That is the reason why you *should* go to church." In my reply, I directed him to Jonathan Edwards' teaching on this important matter. Edwards was probably the strongest predestinarian ever born on American soil, but he developed his doctrine of seeking to help those who ask, "What can I do if it's all up to God?" Edwards replied, "You can seek."

It is important to note that Edwards was not speaking of authentic seeking, the effort of those who are in love with Christ to gain a greater knowledge of Him. But Edwards would say to his people: "You don't know whether you're elect or not elect. You know that if you don't have faith, you're going to go to hell. You know that it is to your advantage to find out whether you have any capacity for faith, and you know that the ordinary way in which God brings people to saving faith is through the preaching of the gospel. So even if you have no love for God whatsoever and only have your own self-interest at heart here—your enlightened self-interest—the wise thing is to put yourself in the way of grace; that is, place yourself where the means of grace are most commonly concentrated, and that means attending the preaching of the Word of God. It is to your advantage to do this even if you find it boring, odious, and distasteful. Perhaps God, in His mercy, will pierce your heart as you are listening to the Word of God."

I believe that is wise advice. If you are not a believer, please do not conclude that there is nothing you can do because you might not be among the elect. There is something you can do about your condition right now. You can go and be where the Word of God is proclaimed, even if your motives are completely selfish. Do that. If you have any wisdom, you'll run to those places.

Strengthening Faith

After affirming that "the grace of faith . . . is ordinarily wrought by the ministry of the Word," the Westminster Confession statement on saving faith adds, "by which also, and by the administration of the sacraments, and prayer, it is increased and strengthened."

Reformed theology never speaks of an increase of justification, because justification rests on the righteousness of Christ, and there's nothing we can do to increase that righteousness or merit. It is already perfect. We cannot add to it and we cannot subtract from it. However, the Bible does speak of faith growing. In fact, it both grows and shrinks (though it can never be destroyed). Our faith in God goes through dry spells, when we cry out, "I believe; help my unbelief" (Mark 9:24). In various seasons, the faith by which we cling to Christ can be stronger or weaker. The writers of the confession were concerned to set forth ways in which it can be strengthened. The faith by which we are saved may be as small as a mustard seed, but that faith, however infinitesimal it may be in its beginning, can grow and become increasingly strong so that we become increasingly productive as Christians.

Not only does the beginning of faith depend on the supernatural grace of God, the strengthening of that faith relies on God's sanctifying grace. What we call the "means of grace," the "tools" by which grace is administered to us, are very important. What are these means?

We've already begun to discuss one of them—the ministry of the Word. The more I expose myself to the Word of God, the greater my faith will be. By the same token, if I am negligent in reading the Scriptures, I open myself to ideas pouring into my head from the secular world, which may lessen the ardor of my faith. I then need to get back into the Word. As I read the Scriptures and say, "Yes, that's true," my soul is stirred up. That's why we need to be in church every Sunday morning and not neglect such gatherings (Heb. 10:24–25). We desperately need these times to focus our attention on the hearing of the Word of God.

If I thought that the fruit of my preaching rested on a single sermon that I preached, I would quit the ministry in abject despair. At one time, I taught an hourlong class every week in a church. Each week I raised a question about what I had taught the week before, and most of the people did not remember what I had said. Unfortunately, in that context I did not have the benefit that I have in the seminary setting of giving assignments so that my students have to read, go over their notes, and digest the material. As a result, most of what those in the church class learned each week they did not retain. If that was the case in an hourlong class, what about a thirty-minute sermon? How much impact does that have on people? Sometimes I can preach a sermon I preached two years earlier, and no one notices. I worry about repetition, but people say: "Oh, you preached that before? We missed that somehow." That is difficult for preachers.

What sustains me is that I know God has chosen preaching as His means to quicken people to faith and to strengthen them in their faith. He has promised that His Word will not return to Him void (Isa. 55:11). Even though many Christians cannot remember three sermons that they have heard in their lives, nevertheless, every time they hear the Word of God—even if their minds wander—the Word of God makes an impact on them. It is a means of grace.

Sacraments and Prayer

The Westminster Confession also indicates that the administration of the sacraments is helpful, because the sacraments of baptism and the Lord's Supper are tangible, demonstrative (nonverbal) communications of the Word of God. They are demonstrations of the truth of the gospel that impact our senses, not just our minds. The sacraments reinforce and strengthen our faith because they reinforce and strengthen the Word of God.

The last thing mentioned in the confession quote on saving faith is prayer. Prayer is one of the most important means of grace that we have to strengthen our faith. Prayer is not for God's benefit. We don't pray to give Him information that otherwise He would not have. We don't pray to give God our counsel so as to improve His administration of the universe. Rather, prayer is for our benefit. It is a God-given way for us to spend time with Him, to praise and thank Him, and to make our requests known to Him. Afterward, when we get up from our knees, we watch the providence of God work in our lives. In short, we see God answering prayers. What does that do to our faith? It strengthens it. That's why prayer is a very important means of grace.

The ministry of the Word of God is vitally important to our faith. This is why the many opponents of the trust-worthiness of sacred Scripture in our day are such a danger to the flock. Even people who supposedly are leaders in the church are cutting off the access of God's people to the most important means of grace they have for strengthening their faith.

You have a choice: You can either listen to the critics of the Bible or you can come to the Scriptures themselves. The Holy Spirit never promises to minister through the words of the critics. But He does minister to your soul through the reading and the studying of His sacred Word.

When you struggle with your faith, when you face the dark night of the soul, when you are not sure of where you stand with the things of God, flee to the Scriptures. It is from those pages that God the Holy Spirit will speak to you, minister to your soul, and strengthen the faith that He gave to you in the first place.

About the Author

Dr. R. C. Sproul is the founder and chairman of Ligonier Ministries, an international multimedia ministry based in Sanford, Florida. He also serves as senior minister of preaching and teaching at Saint Andrew's, a Reformed congregation in Sanford, and as president of Reformation Bible College, and his teaching can be heard around the world on the daily radio program *Renewing Your Mind*.

During his distinguished academic career, Dr. Sproul helped train men for the ministry as a professor at several theological seminaries.

He is the author of more than eighty books, including *The Holiness of God*, *Chosen by God*, *The Invisible Hand*, *Faith Alone*, *A Taste of Heaven*, *Truths We Confess*, *The Truth of the Cross*, and *The Prayer of the Lord*. He also served as general editor of *The Reformation Study Bible* and has written several children's books, including *The Prince's Poison Cup*.

Dr. Sproul and his wife, Vesta, make their home in Longwood, Florida.

Further your Bible study with *Tabletalk* magazine, another learning tool from R.C. Sproul.

....

A Bible study for each day—Bringing the best in biblical scholarship together with down-to-earth writing, *Tabletalk* helps you understand the Bible and apply it to daily living.

Trusted theological resource—*Tabletalk* avoids trends, shallow doctrine and popular movements to present biblical truth simply and clearly.

Corresponding digital edition—Print subscribers have access to the digital edition for iPad, Kindle Fire, and Android tablet devices.

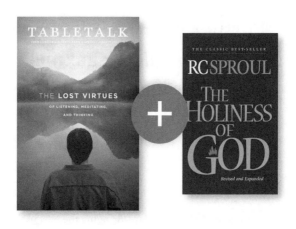

Sign-up for a free, 3-month trial
of *Tabletalk* magazine
and get *The Holiness of God*
by R.C. Sproul for free.

Go online at TryTabletalk.com/CQ